D1404539

Daria Rose
and
The Day She Chose

By

Yvonne Capitelli
Art By Sherri Forrester Baldy

Dear Andie,
Make good choices and always
do your best!

Yvonne
Capitelli

ASunnyDay Publishing 2008

Note to Parents

Words you may want to discuss with your child:

1. Overwhelmed

2. Confidence

3. Situations

4. Faith

5. Stressful

6. Discouraged

7. Succeed

8. Self-control

9. Thankful

10. Determination

Published by ASunnyDay Publishing
Rockville Centre, N.Y. 11570
ypsunnydays@gmail.com

Illustrations by Sherri Forrester Baldy
Graphic design by Paul MacGown

ISBN 978-0-9818366-0-7

First Edition
August 2008

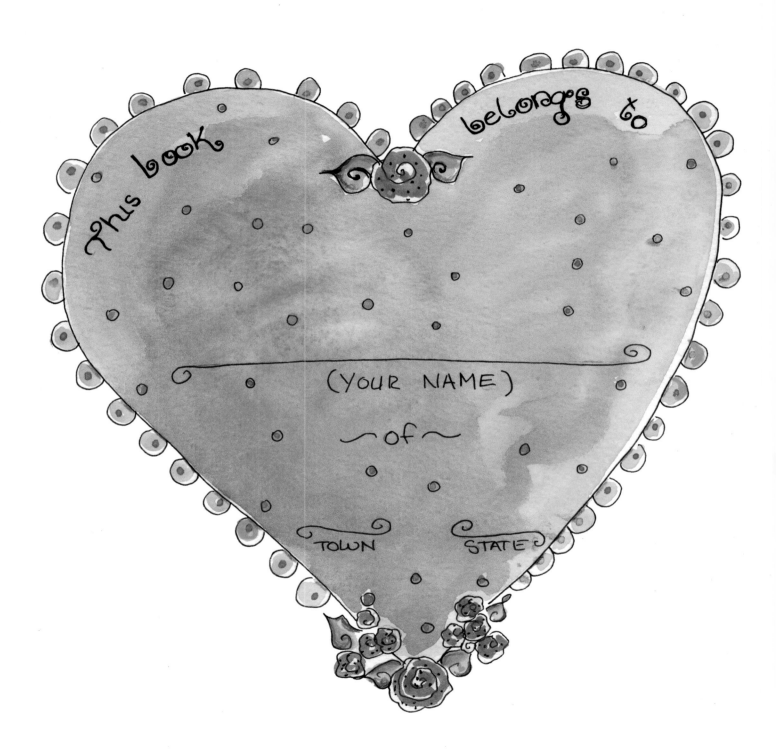

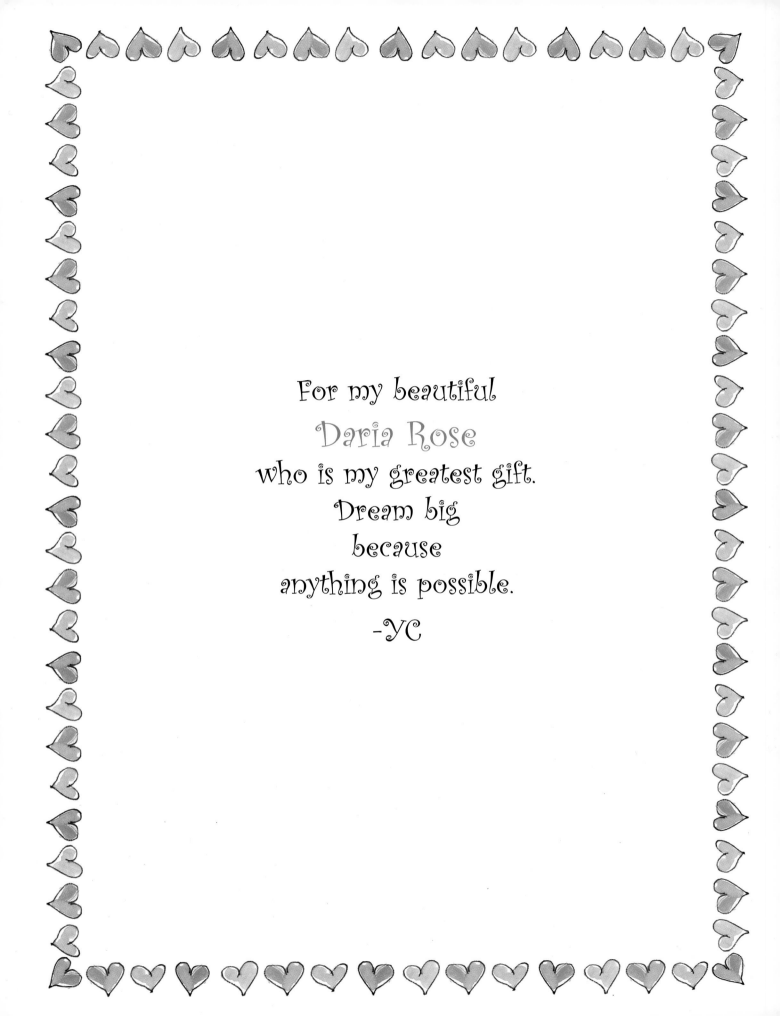

For my beautiful
Daria Rose
who is my greatest gift.
Dream big
because
anything is possible.

-YC

There was a girl named Daria Rose. She was a very kind and loving girl. It was Sunday night before bedtime and Daria Rose was snuggled in her bed waiting for her Mom to come in and say good night. She started thinking about how hard everything seemed. Her schoolwork was getting more difficult. Some of the girls in her class were mean to her. She felt confused and overwhelmed. Sometimes she felt like she just didn't fit in.

When her Mom came in to say good night, she could see Daria Rose was upset.

After Daria Rose finished telling her Mom how she was feeling, her Mom said, "You have the power and control over what your world is like around you. If you believe in yourself, have confidence, and make good choices, then good things will happen all around you."

"You can't change how other people treat you, but you can choose how it makes you feel." Her Mom went on to explain, "What you think and how you act can make even a bad situation turn out good. Don't let being afraid stop you from making the right decisions. Don't let others change how you feel about yourself and how you behave. Think about the happy result you want, what you have to do to make it happen and then do it. Dream big and never ever give up, because anything is possible."

They said their prayers together and Daria Rose's Mom gave her a big kiss and hug and said, "I have faith you will choose the right things to do. I love you more than the moon and all the stars in the sky."

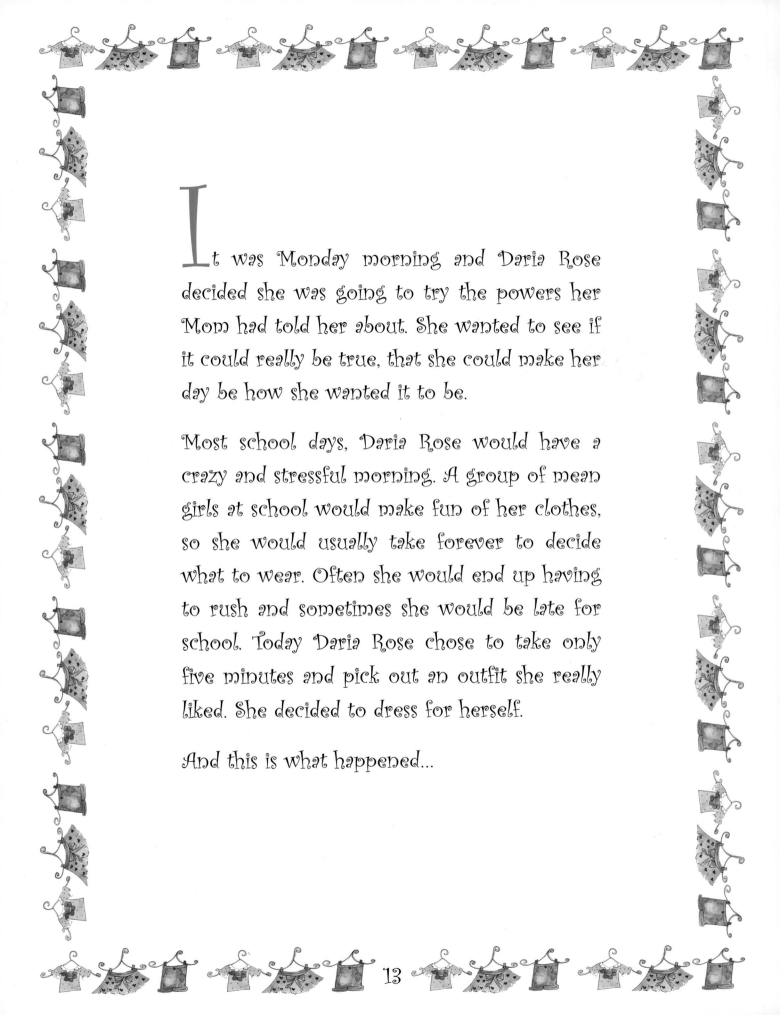

It was Monday morning and Daria Rose decided she was going to try the powers her Mom had told her about. She wanted to see if it could really be true, that she could make her day be how she wanted it to be.

Most school days, Daria Rose would have a crazy and stressful morning. A group of mean girls at school would make fun of her clothes, so she would usually take forever to decide what to wear. Often she would end up having to rush and sometimes she would be late for school. Today Daria Rose chose to take only five minutes and pick out an outfit she really liked. She decided to dress for herself.

And this is what happened...

Because she was ready so fast, she and her Mom enjoyed a very relaxing breakfast. There was no rushing. They talked and laughed and had such a fun morning. The best part was that she was on time for school.

14

On Mondays, Daria took the bus home from school because her Mom had to work. On the ride home, Vicky the bully made fun of Daria's pants. "Your pants are ugly. You don't have cool clothes. What's wrong, don't you have any money?" This time Daria Rose decided not to let it bother her. She chose to understand that Vicky being mean had nothing to do with her. Daria remembered getting dressed, how much she liked her outfit and how great she felt when she looked in the mirror. She decided not to let Vicky change how she felt about herself. Daria took a seat next to her friend Molly and the two laughed and enjoyed the bus ride home.

And this is what happened...

Daria Rose got off the bus with the same smile and confidence she got on with and, of course, her new power of choosing.

On Tuesday, Daria decided to try her powers again. She told herself she was going to have a great day. Last week her teacher, Mr. McQuiggly, told the class he would be giving a science test on Wednesday. Daria Rose had not been doing well on her science tests and she had become very discouraged.

When Daria went home that night she decided she was going to get a good grade. She remembered what her Mom had said, "Have confidence and make good choices and don't let fear stop you. You have to believe you can do well. Have faith and you will succeed. You have the power to see yourself with a good grade and make it happen. It is your choice to do well. You must decide how important it is to you."

Daria Rose studied harder than ever and she had her Mom quiz her. The next day she studied after breakfast and in the car on the way to school.

And this is what happened...

On Wednesday morning, Daria Rose sat at her desk. Mr. McQuiggly handed out the test. Before she began, she closed her eyes and said to herself, "I will get a good grade! I have studied hard. I can do it!" She pictured an A+ on her test. When she was all done she handed in her test. She felt confident that she had done her best.

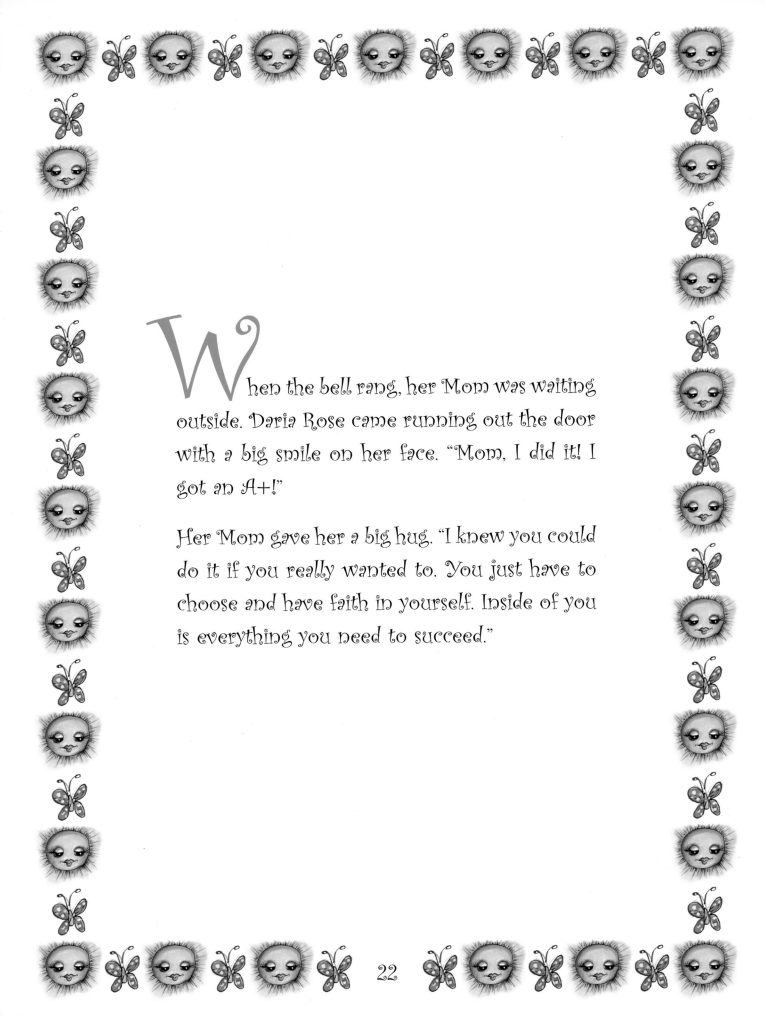

When the bell rang, her Mom was waiting outside. Daria Rose came running out the door with a big smile on her face. "Mom, I did it! I got an A+!"

Her Mom gave her a big hug. "I knew you could do it if you really wanted to. You just have to choose and have faith in yourself. Inside of you is everything you need to succeed."

By Thursday, Daria Rose was feeling very confident. She liked being in control of her days.

On the ride to school she thought of the new girl, Michelle. She wanted to be friends with her, but because the group of mean girls teased Michelle, Daria was afraid. She decided that today she would not be afraid. Today she would make a new friend.

And this is what happened...

During lunch, she overheard the mean girls teasing Michelle who, as usual, was sitting by herself. Daria Rose picked up her tray, walked over and sat down next to Michelle. The mean girls just stared.

Daria asked Michelle, "Is it okay if I eat with you?" Michelle just smiled and nodded yes. They ate and talked as if no one else were in the lunchroom. For the rest of the day, every time she passed Michelle in the hallway, Michelle was smiling. She never realized the power and control that was inside her all along. She felt very happy inside.

On Friday, she couldn't believe the great week she had. Daria Rose decided from now on she would be making smart choices on how all her future days would be. She would no longer let her days be controlled by what others thought or how others behaved. She would make decisions with confidence and not out of fear of what might happen. In each situation she would ask herself these five questions:

1. What do I want to happen?
2. What do I need to do to make it happen?
3. What am I afraid of and what is the worst thing that can happen?
4. Whom could I ask to help me?
5. Will my decision make things better?

On Saturday night while Daria was snuggled in bed, her mind was filled with good thoughts. She had happy thoughts, feelings of good choices and jobs well done. She also felt proud of how she chose to make a new friend. Daria was very grateful for the awesome advice her Mom had given her.

Her Mom came in, they said their prayers and Daria Rose told her of her amazing week. Her Mom smiled and said, "We all make choices and you have learned how to make good ones. You have made yourself happier and the world around you a kinder and better place."

As Daria Rose fell asleep with a smile on her face, her Mom said softly, "I love you more than the moon and all the stars in the sky. Let the butterflies kiss you."

The
End